THE SUPER AUTHOR JOURNAL

BY SHARON C. JENKINS

Copyright © 2022 by Sharon C. Jenkins
All rights reserved. This book or any portion thereof may not be reproduced or used in any manner whatsoever without the express written permission of the publisher except for the use of brief quotations in a book review.
Printed in the United States of America
First Printing, 2022
ISBN 978-1-7354642-1-3

2162 Spring Stuebner Rd., Suite #140 - 1018
Spring, TX 77389
www.mcwritingservices.com

WHAT IS A SUPER AUTHOR?

A super author is someone who masters the art of authorpreneurship.

Author: "a person who makes or originates something; creator; originator. They are a writer of a book, article, blog, etc. An author is a person whose profession is writing books."

Entrepreneur: "a person who organizes and manages a business undertaking, assuming the risk for the sake of the profit."

NOTES

The Master Communicator says…

- Writing is like any other profession, if you want to be at the top of your game you must prepare to do so.
- Preparation and perspiration are often the best tools associated with mastering your craft. It's no different in the writing industry. To sell books you must be good at what you do.

NOTES

What is Authorpreneurship?

- It's not being a better writer
- It's not a "get rich quick" scheme
- It's not for punks!

NOTES

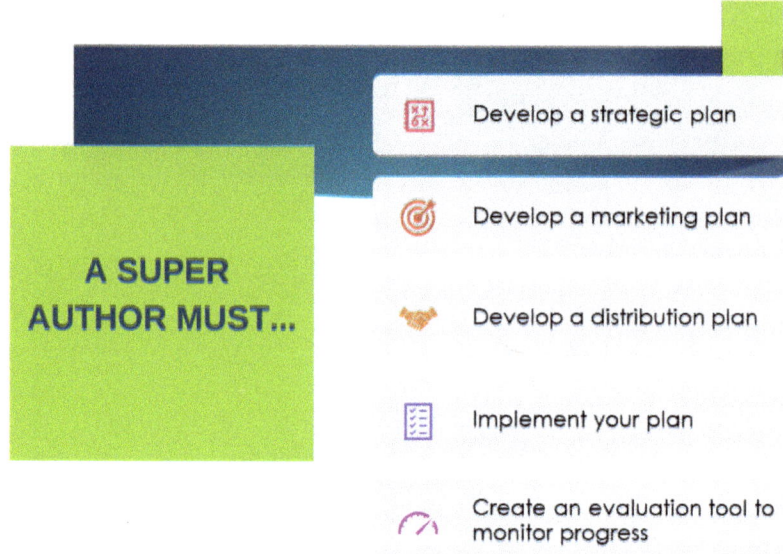

A SUPER AUTHOR MUST...

- Develop a strategic plan
- Develop a marketing plan
- Develop a distribution plan
- Implement your plan
- Create an evaluation tool to monitor progress

NOTES

Elements of Authorpreneurship

- Evaluate your literary assets and liabilities
- Do a marketability analysis
- Do a personal financial assessment
- Create a dream sheet for this literary project
- Establish an advisory team of support professionals

NOTES

Elements of a Start-Up Book Project

- Determine what type of book you are writing
- Determine what the proposed title will be
- Determine the book's premise
- Determine the book's mission
- Determine what the reader will gain from the book

NOTES

Elements of a Start-Up Book Project

- Identify your book's exceptionality
- Identify your target audience
- Determine who is your competition
- Identify your credentials as an expert on the subject matter
- Determine your marketing strategy
- Establish your literally team

NOTES

SUPER AUTHOR RESOURCES

Reading Lists

TITLE	AUTHOR	GENRE	DATE	RATING
				☆☆☆☆☆
				☆☆☆☆☆
				☆☆☆☆☆
				☆☆☆☆☆
				☆☆☆☆☆
				☆☆☆☆☆
				☆☆☆☆☆
				☆☆☆☆☆
				☆☆☆☆☆
				☆☆☆☆☆
				☆☆☆☆☆
				☆☆☆☆☆
				☆☆☆☆☆
				☆☆☆☆☆
				☆☆☆☆☆
				☆☆☆☆☆
				☆☆☆☆☆
				☆☆☆☆☆
				☆☆☆☆☆
				☆☆☆☆☆
				☆☆☆☆☆
				☆☆☆☆☆
				☆☆☆☆☆

Reading Lists

TITLE	AUTHOR	GENRE	DATE	RATING
				☆☆☆☆☆
				☆☆☆☆☆
				☆☆☆☆☆
				☆☆☆☆☆
				☆☆☆☆☆
				☆☆☆☆☆
				☆☆☆☆☆
				☆☆☆☆☆
				☆☆☆☆☆
				☆☆☆☆☆
				☆☆☆☆☆
				☆☆☆☆☆
				☆☆☆☆☆
				☆☆☆☆☆
				☆☆☆☆☆
				☆☆☆☆☆
				☆☆☆☆☆
				☆☆☆☆☆
				☆☆☆☆☆
				☆☆☆☆☆
				☆☆☆☆☆
				☆☆☆☆☆
				☆☆☆☆☆

Reading Lists

TITLE	AUTHOR	GENRE	DATE	RATING
				☆☆☆☆☆
				☆☆☆☆☆
				☆☆☆☆☆
				☆☆☆☆☆
				☆☆☆☆☆
				☆☆☆☆☆
				☆☆☆☆☆
				☆☆☆☆☆
				☆☆☆☆☆
				☆☆☆☆☆
				☆☆☆☆☆
				☆☆☆☆☆
				☆☆☆☆☆
				☆☆☆☆☆
				☆☆☆☆☆
				☆☆☆☆☆
				☆☆☆☆☆
				☆☆☆☆☆
				☆☆☆☆☆
				☆☆☆☆☆
				☆☆☆☆☆
				☆☆☆☆☆
				☆☆☆☆☆

Reading Lists

TITLE	AUTHOR	GENRE	DATE	RATING
				☆☆☆☆☆
				☆☆☆☆☆
				☆☆☆☆☆
				☆☆☆☆☆
				☆☆☆☆☆
				☆☆☆☆☆
				☆☆☆☆☆
				☆☆☆☆☆
				☆☆☆☆☆
				☆☆☆☆☆
				☆☆☆☆☆
				☆☆☆☆☆
				☆☆☆☆☆
				☆☆☆☆☆
				☆☆☆☆☆
				☆☆☆☆☆
				☆☆☆☆☆
				☆☆☆☆☆
				☆☆☆☆☆
				☆☆☆☆☆
				☆☆☆☆☆
				☆☆☆☆☆
				☆☆☆☆☆
				☆☆☆☆☆

Reading Lists

TITLE	AUTHOR	GENRE	DATE	RATING
				☆☆☆☆☆
				☆☆☆☆☆
				☆☆☆☆☆
				☆☆☆☆☆
				☆☆☆☆☆
				☆☆☆☆☆
				☆☆☆☆☆
				☆☆☆☆☆
				☆☆☆☆☆
				☆☆☆☆☆
				☆☆☆☆☆
				☆☆☆☆☆
				☆☆☆☆☆
				☆☆☆☆☆
				☆☆☆☆☆
				☆☆☆☆☆
				☆☆☆☆☆
				☆☆☆☆☆
				☆☆☆☆☆
				☆☆☆☆☆
				☆☆☆☆☆
				☆☆☆☆☆
				☆☆☆☆☆
				☆☆☆☆☆

DAY PLANNER

Date: _____

M T W Th F Sa Su

To Do

_____
_____
_____
_____
_____
_____
_____
_____
_____
_____
_____
_____

Priorities

Enthusiastic for

Appointments

_____
_____
_____
_____

Breakfast	Lunch	Dinner	Snack

Fitness	Mood

DAY PLANNER

Date: _____

M T W Th F Sa Su

To Do

_____
_____
_____
_____
_____
_____
_____
_____
_____
_____
_____
_____

Priorities

Enthusiastic for

Appointments

_____
_____
_____
_____
_____

Breakfast	Lunch	Dinner	Snack

Fitness	Mood

DAY PLANNER

Date: _____

M T W Th F Sa Su

To Do

_____
_____
_____
_____
_____
_____
_____
_____
_____
_____
_____
_____
_____

Priorities

Enthusiastic for

Appointments

_____
_____
_____
_____
_____

Breakfast	Lunch	Dinner	Snack

Fitness	Mood

DAY PLANNER

Date: _____

M T W Th F Sa Su

To Do

Priorities

Enthusiastic for

Appointments

| Breakfast | Lunch | Dinner | Snack |

| Fitness | Mood |

DAY PLANNER

Date: _____

M　T　W　Th　F　Sa　Su

To Do

Priorities

Enthusiastic for

Appointments

Breakfast	Lunch	Dinner	Snack

Fitness	Mood

DAY PLANNER

Date: _____

M T W Th F Sa Su

To Do

_____
_____
_____
_____
_____
_____
_____
_____
_____
_____
_____
_____

Priorities

Enthusiastic for

Appointments

_____
_____
_____
_____
_____

Breakfast	Lunch	Dinner	Snack

Fitness	Mood

DAY PLANNER

Date: _____

M   T   W   Th   F   Sa   Su

To Do

_____
_____
_____
_____
_____
_____
_____
_____
_____
_____
_____
_____

Priorities

Enthusiastic for

Appointments

_____
_____
_____
_____

Breakfast	Lunch	Dinner	Snack

Fitness	Mood

Weekly Planner

Monday

Tuesday

Wednesday

Thursday

Friday

Saturday

Sunday

To-do

Notes

Weekly Planner

Monday

Tuesday

Wednesday

Thursday

Friday

Saturday

Sunday

to-do

Notes

Weekly Planner

Monday

Tuesday

Wednesday

Thursday

Friday

Saturday

Sunday

to-do

Notes

Weekly Planner

Monday

Tuesday

Wednesday

Thursday

Friday

Saturday

Sunday

to-do

Notes

Weekly Planner

Monday

Tuesday

Wednesday

Thursday

Friday

Saturday

Sunday

To-do

Notes

Monthly Planner

Month: _____ **Year:** _____

Monday	Tuesday	Wednesday	Thursday	Friday	Saturday	Sunday
☐	☐	☐	☐	☐	☐	☐
☐	☐	☐	☐	☐	☐	☐
☐	☐	☐	☐	☐	☐	☐
☐	☐	☐	☐	☐	☐	☐
☐	☐	☐	☐	☐	☐	☐

Notes:

Monthly Planner

Month: _____ **Year:** _____

Monday	Tuesday	Wednesday	Thursday	Friday	Saturday	Sunday
☐	☐	☐	☐	☐	☐	☐
☐	☐	☐	☐	☐	☐	☐
☐	☐	☐	☐	☐	☐	☐
☐	☐	☐	☐	☐	☐	☐
☐	☐	☐	☐	☐	☐	☐

Notes:

_____
_____
_____
_____
_____
_____
_____
_____

Monthly Planner

Month: _____ **Year:** _____

Monday	Tuesday	Wednesday	Thursday	Friday	Saturday	Sunday
☐	☐	☐	☐	☐	☐	☐
☐	☐	☐	☐	☐	☐	☐
☐	☐	☐	☐	☐	☐	☐
☐	☐	☐	☐	☐	☐	☐
☐	☐	☐	☐	☐	☐	☐

Notes:

_____
_____
_____
_____
_____
_____
_____

Monthly Planner

Month: _____ **Year:** _____

Monday	Tuesday	Wednesday	Thursday	Friday	Saturday	Sunday
☐	☐	☐	☐	☐	☐	☐
☐	☐	☐	☐	☐	☐	☐
☐	☐	☐	☐	☐	☐	☐
☐	☐	☐	☐	☐	☐	☐
☐	☐	☐	☐	☐	☐	☐

Notes:
_____
_____
_____
_____
_____
_____
_____
_____

Monthly Planner

Month: _____ **Year:** _____

Monday	Tuesday	Wednesday	Thursday	Friday	Saturday	Sunday
☐	☐	☐	☐	☐	☐	☐
☐	☐	☐	☐	☐	☐	☐
☐	☐	☐	☐	☐	☐	☐
☐	☐	☐	☐	☐	☐	☐
☐	☐	☐	☐	☐	☐	☐

Notes:

_____
_____
_____
_____
_____
_____
_____
_____

Monthly Planner

Month: _____ Year: _____

Monday	Tuesday	Wednesday	Thursday	Friday	Saturday	Sunday
☐	☐	☐	☐	☐	☐	☐
☐	☐	☐	☐	☐	☐	☐
☐	☐	☐	☐	☐	☐	☐
☐	☐	☐	☐	☐	☐	☐
☐	☐	☐	☐	☐	☐	☐

Notes:
_____
_____
_____
_____
_____
_____
_____
_____

Monthly Planner

Month: _____ **Year:** _____

Monday	Tuesday	Wednesday	Thursday	Friday	Saturday	Sunday
☐	☐	☐	☐	☐	☐	☐
☐	☐	☐	☐	☐	☐	☐
☐	☐	☐	☐	☐	☐	☐
☐	☐	☐	☐	☐	☐	☐
☐	☐	☐	☐	☐	☐	☐

Notes:

_____
_____
_____
_____
_____
_____
_____
_____

Monthly Planner

Month: _____ **Year:** _____

Monday	Tuesday	Wednesday	Thursday	Friday	Saturday	Sunday
☐	☐	☐	☐	☐	☐	☐
☐	☐	☐	☐	☐	☐	☐
☐	☐	☐	☐	☐	☐	☐
☐	☐	☐	☐	☐	☐	☐
☐	☐	☐	☐	☐	☐	☐

Notes:
_____
_____
_____
_____
_____
_____
_____
_____

Monthly Planner

Month: _____ **Year:** _____

Monday	Tuesday	Wednesday	Thursday	Friday	Saturday	Sunday
☐	☐	☐	☐	☐	☐	☐
☐	☐	☐	☐	☐	☐	☐
☐	☐	☐	☐	☐	☐	☐
☐	☐	☐	☐	☐	☐	☐
☐	☐	☐	☐	☐	☐	☐

Notes:

_____
_____
_____
_____
_____
_____
_____
_____

Monthly Planner

Month: _____ **Year:** _____

Monday	Tuesday	Wednesday	Thursday	Friday	Saturday	Sunday
☐	☐	☐	☐	☐	☐	☐
☐	☐	☐	☐	☐	☐	☐
☐	☐	☐	☐	☐	☐	☐
☐	☐	☐	☐	☐	☐	☐
☐	☐	☐	☐	☐	☐	☐

Notes:

_____
_____
_____
_____
_____
_____
_____
_____

Monthly Planner

Month: _____ **Year:** _____

Monday	Tuesday	Wednesday	Thursday	Friday	Saturday	Sunday
☐	☐	☐	☐	☐	☐	☐
☐	☐	☐	☐	☐	☐	☐
☐	☐	☐	☐	☐	☐	☐
☐	☐	☐	☐	☐	☐	☐
☐	☐	☐	☐	☐	☐	☐

Notes:
_____
_____
_____
_____
_____
_____
_____
_____

Monthly Planner

Month: _____ Year: _____

Monday	Tuesday	Wednesday	Thursday	Friday	Saturday	Sunday
☐	☐	☐	☐	☐	☐	☐
☐	☐	☐	☐	☐	☐	☐
☐	☐	☐	☐	☐	☐	☐
☐	☐	☐	☐	☐	☐	☐
☐	☐	☐	☐	☐	☐	☐

Notes:
_____
_____
_____
_____
_____
_____
_____
_____
_____

MONTHLY TO-DO LIST

JANUARY
- [ ]
- [ ]
- [ ]
- [ ]
- [ ]

FEBRUARY
- [ ]
- [ ]
- [ ]
- [ ]
- [ ]

MARCH
- [ ]
- [ ]
- [ ]
- [ ]
- [ ]

APRIL
- [ ]
- [ ]
- [ ]
- [ ]
- [ ]

MAY
- [ ]
- [ ]
- [ ]
- [ ]
- [ ]

JUNE
- [ ]
- [ ]
- [ ]
- [ ]
- [ ]

JULY
- [ ]
- [ ]
- [ ]
- [ ]
- [ ]

AUGUST
- [ ]
- [ ]
- [ ]
- [ ]
- [ ]

SEPTEMBER
- [ ]
- [ ]
- [ ]
- [ ]
- [ ]

OCTOBER
- [ ]
- [ ]
- [ ]
- [ ]
- [ ]

NOVEMBER
- [ ]
- [ ]
- [ ]
- [ ]
- [ ]

DECEMBER
- [ ]
- [ ]
- [ ]
- [ ]
- [ ]

Project to complete

project	
deadline	completed ☐

items required · tasks to-do

project	
deadline	completed ☐

items required · tasks to-do

Project to complete

project	
deadline	completed ☐

items required   tasks to-do

---

project	
deadline	completed ☐

items required   tasks to-do

Project to complete

project	
deadline	completed ☐

items required · tasks to-do

project	
deadline	completed ☐

items required · tasks to-do

Project to complete

project	
deadline	completed ☐

items required | tasks to-do

project	
deadline	completed ☐

items required | tasks to-do

Project to complete

project	
deadline	completed ☐

items required / tasks to-do

---

project	
deadline	completed ☐

items required / tasks to-do

Project to complete

project	
deadline	completed ☐

items required / tasks to-do

project	
deadline	completed ☐

items required / tasks to-do

Project to complete

project	
deadline	completed ☐

items required   tasks to-do

project	
deadline	completed ☐

items required   tasks to-do

Project to complete

project	
deadline	completed ☐

items required · tasks to-do

project	
deadline	completed ☐

items required · tasks to-do

Project to complete

project	
deadline	completed ☐

items required   tasks to-do

project	
deadline	completed ☐

items required   tasks to-do

Project to complete

project	
deadline	completed ☐

items required   **tasks to-do**

---

project	
deadline	completed ☐

items required   **tasks to-do**

Project Name: Priority: ☐ ☐ ☐ ☐ ☐

Date: Difficulty: ☐ ☐ ☐ ☐ ☐

Description: Ideas:

Materials:
☐
☐
☐
☐
☐
☐
☐
☐
☐
☐

Sketches:

Notes:

Project Name: Priority: ☐ ☐ ☐ ☐ ☐

Date: Difficulty: ☐ ☐ ☐ ☐ ☐

Description:

Ideas:

Materials:

☐
☐
☐
☐
☐
☐
☐
☐
☐
☐

Sketches:

Notes:

Project Name: Priority: ☐ ☐ ☐ ☐ ☐

Date: Difficulty: ☐ ☐ ☐ ☐ ☐

Description:

Ideas:

Materials:

☐ _____
☐ _____
☐ _____
☐ _____
☐ _____
☐ _____
☐ _____
☐ _____
☐ _____
☐ _____

Sketches:

Notes:

Project Name: Priority: ☐ ☐ ☐ ☐ ☐

Date: Difficulty: ☐ ☐ ☐ ☐ ☐

Description:

Ideas:

Materials:

☐ _____
☐ _____
☐ _____
☐ _____
☐ _____
☐ _____
☐ _____
☐ _____
☐ _____
☐ _____

Sketches:

Notes:

Project Name: Priority: ☐ ☐ ☐ ☐ ☐

Date: Difficulty: ☐ ☐ ☐ ☐ ☐

Description:

Ideas:

Materials:

☐
☐
☐
☐
☐
☐
☐
☐
☐
☐

Sketches:

Notes:

Project Name: Priority: ☐ ☐ ☐ ☐ ☐
Date: Difficulty: ☐ ☐ ☐ ☐ ☐

Description: Ideas:

_____

_____

_____

_____

_____

Materials:

☐ _____
☐ _____
☐ _____
☐ _____
☐ _____   Sketches:
☐ _____
☐ _____
☐ _____
☐ _____
☐ _____

Notes:

_____

_____

_____

_____

_____

Project Name: Priority: ☐ ☐ ☐ ☐

Date: Difficulty: ☐ ☐ ☐ ☐

Description: Ideas:

Materials:
☐
☐
☐
☐
☐
☐
☐
☐
☐
☐

Sketches:

Notes:

Project Name: Priority: ☐ ☐ ☐ ☐ ☐
Date: Difficulty: ☐ ☐ ☐ ☐ ☐

Description:

Ideas:

Materials:
☐
☐
☐
☐
☐
☐
☐
☐
☐
☐

Sketches:

Notes:

Project Name: Priority: ☐ ☐ ☐ ☐ ☐

Date: Difficulty: ☐ ☐ ☐ ☐ ☐

Description:

Ideas:

Materials:
- ☐
- ☐
- ☐
- ☐
- ☐
- ☐
- ☐
- ☐
- ☐
- ☐

Sketches:

Notes:

Project Name: Priority: ☐ ☐ ☐ ☐ ☐

Date: Difficulty: ☐ ☐ ☐ ☐ ☐

Description: Ideas:

_____
_____
_____
_____
_____
_____

Materials:

☐ _____
☐ _____
☐ _____
☐ _____
☐ _____
☐ _____
☐ _____
☐ _____
☐ _____
☐ _____

Sketches:

Notes:

_____
_____
_____
_____
_____
_____

TO-DO LIST

TO-DO LIST

TO-DO LIST

TO-DO LIST

TO-DO LIST

TO-DO LIST

TO-DO LIST

TO-DO LIST

TO-DO LIST

TO-DO LIST

-
-
-
-
-
-
-
-
-
-
-
-
-

- Self Care -

This Week Moto _____

Self-Care Practices	Mon	Tue	Wen	Thu	Fri	Sat	Sun

- Self Care -

This Week Moto _____

_____

Self-Care Practices	Mon	Tue	Wen	Thu	Fri	Sat	Sun

- Self Care -

This Week Moto _____

Self-Care Practices	Mon	Tue	Wen	Thu	Fri	Sat	Sun

- Self Care -

This Week Moto _____

Self-Care Practices	Mon	Tue	Wen	Thu	Fri	Sat	Sun

- Self Care -

This Week Moto _____

Self-Care Practices	Mon	Tue	Wen	Thu	Fri	Sat	Sun

- Self Care -

This Week Moto _____

_____

Self-Care Practices	Mon	Tue	Wen	Thu	Fri	Sat	Sun

- Self Care -

This Week Moto _____

Self-Care Practices	Mon	Tue	Wen	Thu	Fri	Sat	Sun

- Self Care -

This Week Moto _____

Self-Care Practices	Mon	Tue	Wen	Thu	Fri	Sat	Sun

- Self Care -

This Week Moto _____

Self-Care Practices	Mon	Tue	Wen	Thu	Fri	Sat	Sun

- Self Care -

This Week Moto _____

Self-Care Practices	Mon	Tue	Wen	Thu	Fri	Sat	Sun

YOU ARE A SUPER AUTHOR!

www.ingramcontent.com/pod-product-compliance
Lightning Source LLC
Chambersburg PA
CBHW061209070526
44583CB00025B/3171